T0394940

Fun with Opposites

Wet and Dry

by Amy McDonald

BELLWETHER MEDIA
MINNEAPOLIS, MN

BLASTOFF!
Beginners

Blastoff! Beginners are developed by literacy experts and educators to meet the needs of early readers. These engaging informational texts support young children as they begin reading about their world. Through simple language and high frequency words paired with crisp, colorful photos, Blastoff! Beginners launch young readers into the universe of independent reading.

Blastoff! Universe ★

Reading Level — Grade K

Grades 1-3

Grade 4

Sight Words in This Book 🔍

a	get	it	they	your
about	him	of	up	
and	in	on	water	
are	is	the	we	

This edition first published in 2026 by Bellwether Media, Inc.

No part of this publication may be reproduced in whole or in part without written permission of the publisher. For information regarding permission, write to Bellwether Media, Inc., Attention: Permissions Department, 3500 American Blvd W, Suite 150, Bloomington, MN 55431.

Library of Congress Cataloging-in-Publication Data

LC record for Wet and Dry available at: https://lccn.loc.gov/2025003229

Text copyright © 2026 by Bellwether Media, Inc. BLASTOFF! BEGINNERS and associated logos are trademarks and/or registered trademarks of Bellwether Media, Inc. Bellwether Media is a division of FlutterBee Education Group.

Editor: Rebecca Sabelko   Designer: Laura Sowers

Printed in the United States of America, North Mankato, MN.

Table of Contents

Washing the Dog

The dog is wet.
We dry him
after bathtime.

Two Opposites

Wet and dry tell about **moisture**.

Wet means
full of water.

Dry means without water.

Wet and Dry Things

Mud is wet.
Dirt is dry.

dirt

mud

Milk is wet.
We put it on
dry cereal.

milk

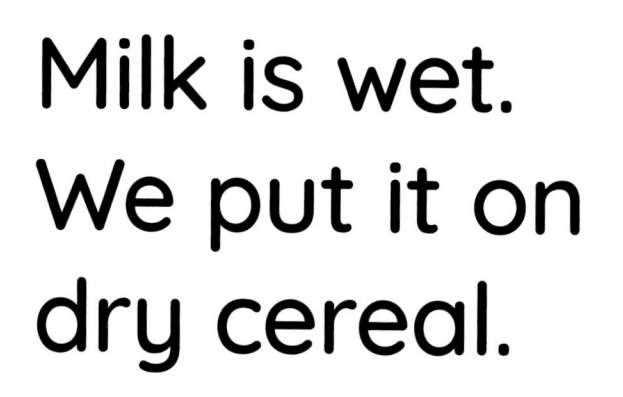

They spilled water.
A dry towel
soaks it up.

The clothes are **damp**. They get dry in the sun.

Think of your favorite weather. Is it wet or dry?

Wet and Dry Facts

Wet and Dry Around Us

dry towel

wet dog

Something Wet and Dry

mud

dirt

Glossary

damp

slightly wet

moisture

water that is in or on something

soaks

takes in water

To Learn More

ON THE WEB

FACTSURFER

Factsurfer.com gives you a safe, fun way to find more information.

1. Go to www.factsurfer.com.

2. Enter "wet and dry" into the search box and click 🔍.

3. Select your book cover to see a list of related content.

Index